A
7-DAY
HEALING &
TRANSFORMATION
DEVOTIONAL

TACONDRA L. BROWN

Table of Contents

Position Your Heart

Hey beautiful, I hope you're ready to explore this devotional for the next seven days with me! After listening to the intro healing song, prayerfully, you have welcomed the Holy Spirit and permitted Him to have His way concerning you. Regardless of your condition, it is my prayer that the fallow ground of your heart be broken, fertile, and ready to receive seeds of healing and transformation. Those seeds being the transforming word of God that has the power to cut, cover, heal, and make you whole. I was pondering over what more I could give to encourage you along the way of your journey. Well, the messages, scriptures, and songs throughout this devotional will serve as leaves to nourish your spirit and heal your soul on your journey, as it did for me. These songs, scriptures, and words of hope and inspiration were given to me by the Holy Spirit and carried me through times when I was struggling to understand what real freedom is, and to embrace my healing. If you are in the middle of a struggle or coming out of one, this devotional will inspire and give you hope to get through it and help someone else overcome for God's glory! If you're not much of a reader, I encourage you to first create a playlist with all the songs mentioned in this devotional and listen to them daily as they will minister to your soul and rejuvenate your spirit. Regardless of where you are in your transformational journey, feeding on these scriptures is a small part of preparing you through this process.

I know the fight of relinquishing one form for the other; however, surrendering the old you for the new version of you is so beautiful and rewarding. Here is a precious pearl to keep with you: As God heals and matures you from the inside out focus more on giving Him praise than complaints. There may be times when you don't hear Him speaking but remember that He's always working and watching! No matter your current season, God knows what He's doing in you and your life! He is the Potter and you are the clay. He is the Author and Finisher of your faith and story! Don't forget to share this and your testimony because others are waiting to be free just like you!

I love you!

Day 1

"For you formed my inward parts; you covered me in my mother's womb. I will praise You, for I am fearfully and wonderfully made."

Psalms 139:14 NKJV

BEAUTIFULLY FORMED

You are a masterpiece! Yes, you! How do I know? Because God doesn't make mistakes! Abba Father knows everything about you. He formed you in secret and fashioned every detail concerning you and His plan for your life. Not even the parents God gave you were a mistake. He knew precisely the DNA required to craft you for His purpose on this earth. To top it off, all of this happened in the complete darkness of your mother's womb, yet, His eyes saw the very core of who you were, who you are, and who you would be. Nothing was hidden from God then, and there's nothing you can cover from Him now. So, stop trying to cover your brokenness because God sees you. If you struggle with a lack of faith or are bound by guilt and shame, God sees you. He sees exactly where you are and is very much aware of what you're going through. The same way our Heavenly Father fashioned the metamorphosis of the butterfly, He also has a process in mind for you to become all He's destined you to be. Your journey may not look like mine or anyone else's, but our overall purpose is to become mature sons of God! To glorify Him in all that we do, and our destination is to spend eternity with Him! This journey of faith isn't always comfortable, and He never promised it would be.

You'll encounter moments of darkness, devastating loss, trials, tribulations, heartaches and pain along the way, but remember God is faithful. He'll never leave or forsake you. He loves you, and that's a promise. Somehow, life has a way of making us forget who we are and whose we are. During, what I like to call, "lonely caterpillar and dark cocoon stages" we tend to forget that no matter what we endure that tries to thwart our progress we were never meant to stay the same. But we were destined to fly from the beginning. Our adversary-the devil- works overtime to make us doubt the power inside of us, and to think that what we carry has no value. The devil's objective is to make you believe you are fatherless, abandoned, forsaken, that God made a mistake when He formed you and you're unfit based on your condition. The enemy is a liar! Guard your heart because he will always attack it the most! Why? Because with the heart we *believe* unto righteousness (*see Romans 10:10).* The heart is where your belief resides and is the key to manifestation. We aren't perfect people, but we were created in the hands of perfection. Real transformation is an inside-out-process; not the opposite as the world deems. It's a matter of your heart being changed, your mind renewed and transformed inwardly before an outward change in appearance ever occurs. Although the caterpillar is not born a butterfly, God designed it to turn into the beautiful creature He created it to be. Transformation is one of the most complex, remarkable processes ever crafted by God and guess what, so is yours.

Psalms 139:13-18, Genesis 1:26-27;31

Has the enemy deceived you into believing you aren't enough or you're living without purpose? Let Holy Spirit lead you into the truth by identifying every root that birthed lies of inadequacy and confront them with the truth of God's word!

"Wonderfully Made" (Ellie Holcomb)
"Journal" (Casey J - The Truth)
"Daddy's Home" (Travis Greene)

Remember This...
YOU ARE FEARFULLY AND WONDERFULLY MADE

Day 2

"Yet I still dare to hope when I remember this: The faithful love of the LORD never ends! His mercies never cease."

Lamentations 3:21-22 (NLT)

BEAUTIFUL HOPE

If you've suffered a loss or experienced a series of traumatic events, you might agree that they can strip you of hope, joy, peace, and cause you to forget what former achievements, sensations, and triumphant moments in life feel like. In so many ways, we could relate to Jeremiah, the Prophet, who wrote the book of Lamentations, also known as "the weeping prophet." Loss can deprive you of optimism, hope for your future, the desire to dream, or even imagine endless possibilities. Instead, it embeds seeds of resentment and bitterness towards

13

people and God in the soil of our hearts. This often happens when your hope is misplaced in people, including yourself, jobs, material things, idols, or false gods than it is in the love and faithfulness of our Heavenly Father.

If you don't believe this to be true, who is often the first person we get angry with, question, turn away from, or feel abandoned by after experiencing hurt, pain, loss, or rejection? God, right? Because *how could a loving, caring, sharing Heavenly Father allow such things to happen to us,* right? That's the question we often ask hastily but hesitate to get the truth about. So, here's the fact. We can't live life avoiding loss, pain, problems, unfavorable circumstances, and people, but we can prepare for them and trust God through it all.

Today's devotional may seem out of place, considering I'm asking you to restore your hope in the Lord after possibly suffering so much pain. You probably want a valid reason as to *why* you should trust Him. But believe me, it's best to start trusting, accepting, and hoping again, now! New hope does not disappoint, because the love of God has been poured out in our hearts by the Holy Spirit, who was given to us. This hope and joy I speak of was given to you and me when received our salvation. You may have lost the joy of your salvation, but it's time to get it back! You have something to patiently and confidently look forward to! I leave you today with this hope: "Yet what we suffer now is nothing compared to the glory He will reveal to us later." (Romans 8:18, NLT).

Lamentations 3: 17-26, Jeremiah 17: 5-8

Take a moment to answer these questions: When did you lose hope? What happened? Who failed you? Is your hope misplaced as a result of your loss? Did you empty your hope into man? Possessions? People? Pleasures? Don't be afraid to remember and don't fear being honest with God about your hurt, anger, and frustrations because He already knows.

Once you address the root, then the fruit in your life can be remedied. Restore your hope in the Lord Jesus Christ today! What a beautiful hope He is! **SAY THIS**: I AM blessed because I trust in the Lord and He is my hope! I am like a tree planted by the waters, and my roots are spread out by the river. I will not fear when the heat of adversity comes; but my leaves will be green, and I will not be anxious in years of drought, nor will I cease from yielding fruit!

"**Better**" (Jessica Reedy)

"**Trust in Me Now**" (Anthony Evans, HOME)

Day 3

"As the clay is in the potter's hand, so are you in my hand."

Jeremiah 18:6 NLT

BEAUTIFULLY BROKEN

The Lord told Jeremiah to go down to the Potter's house, and He would speak to him there. When Jeremiah went, he found the Potter working at the wheel, but the vessel he was making did not turn out as he hoped, so he crushed it into a lump of clay again and started over. When was the last time you went to *The Potter's* house to speak to your Creator about you? Have you yielded to His process of molding and shaping you into His image and likeness? Surrendering and trusting your heart to the hands of our Creator isn't always easy after frequently being crushed and mishandled in the hands of people. God knows and understands this, but you must realize that He is not like the people who hurt you. *God won't break you to be broken*; He *breaks you to be better.*

I learned the hard way that falling upon the stone is the best way to be broken. The Chief Cornerstone is Jesus Christ. You don't have to fear your life being crushed into powder because you refuse to submit if you willingly throw yourself upon Him. You see, God will not break you against your own will, but when you yield to His hand, you'll find there is beauty on the other side of His brokenness. Brokenness is the prerequisite for holiness and true repentance. Brokenness is the process by which our will becomes one with the Father, our desires align with His, and we are made into His image and likeness. I was once like a cracked glass.

In a state of brokenness struggling to keep myself together instead of falling upon the

Stone, shattering, and allowing God to make me whole again. If you ever overflow a cracked glass with water, it would rupture when filled beyond its point of brokenness. So it is with you. The Lord wants to fill you with more of His spirit, but He can only fill you to the level that your earthly brokenness ends. Don't hold on to the fragments of your pain out of fear of being shattered beyond repair.

Beloved, God is a restorer. Sometimes we don't want to release the hurt, unforgiveness, anger, and bitterness that's damaged us, but until God heals those cracks, you will remain at the same level of spiritual immaturity you are; bound by this world's brokenness as your Spirit thirsts for freedom. Now is the time to be healed and set free, but are you ready? Are you as clay prepared for the refining fire? We often want the purpose and promises of God, but we refuse to welcome His processing and pruning in our lives because it shatters our comfort. God only prunes branches that are connected to Him that bear fruit! So if you want to bear much fruit, humbly embrace a lifestyle of pruning. It's uncomfortable, it hurts. Ask God what about you needs changing and surrender to Him daily. When God is preparing you as a vessel of honor, and things don't turn out right in your heart, spirit, or mind the way He hoped, then He must crush you into a ball of clay again and start over. This crushing doesn't always feel good, but it's for your good, and it's all done safely in The Potter's hand! I pray that you will fully understand the beauty of brokenness God's way. Fixing yourself isn't an option because God already has the final masterpiece you are in His mind. Allow Him to mold you into a vessel of honor suitable for His glory.

Jeremiah 18:6, Matthew 21:23-44

HEALING JOURNAL ACTIVITY

What is God constantly trying to break in you that you keep resisting? Is your heart hardened? Why is God's way of brokenness best for you?

HEALING SONGS

"Gracefully Broken" (Tasha Cobbs)
"Let Praises Rise" (Todd Gallberth)
"Joy" (VaShawn Mitchell)

Remember This...

THERE IS BEAUTY IN YOUR BROKENNESS

Day 4

"There is no fear in love, but perfect love drives out fear, because fear expects punishment. The person who is afraid has not been made perfect in love."

1 John 4:18 (CEB)

BEAUTIFULLY LOVED

I never understood the depth of God's love for me because I was blinded by the decaying thoughts that whispered *God doesn't love you.* I believed God was punishing me with pain and suffering for not being good enough and for not successfully meeting the requirements to be a real *child of God*. Do not fall for the enemy's lie that God doesn't love you; that you are inadequate, not good enough, or that you don't meet some standard to be a child of God. That is a lie! The enemy's focus is to get you to doubt God's trustworthiness and love, but you must trust in Him wholeheartedly and believe His love for you is unconditional! There is nothing you must do to earn God's love, and there's nothing you can do to turn His love away. God gives love freely because *HE IS LOVE*. It's His nature. God loved you so much that He sent His Son, Jesus, to die for you and your sins! Now that's love! Would you sacrifice your only child for the freedom of others? Would you sacrifice your own life? I don't know if I could, that's why I'm so grateful HE DID. Whom the Son sets free is free indeed! If we only believed this scripture with our hearts and knew what freedom looked and felt like, for real, we'd live life more abundantly as promised. Often, we fear giving God full access to our heart when there is pain, unforgiveness, bitterness, and anger rooted in our soul due to bad past experiences and broken trust. If you continuously feel like God is punishing you and you think you deserve it, or if you believe it's healthy to expect the worst, then you have not fully experienced God's perfect love because of fear. God is love, and there is no fear in love. Fear kills love. Fear is an enemy of the soul (*a stronghold*) the enemy uses to create distance between God and us and to deter us from the *truth*, being Jesus Christ. Beloved, God did not create you to fear. He created you to love you and for you to worship Him! The adversary wants you to spend life entangled in fear, disbelief, and distrust, not knowing who you indeed are and trying to protect yourself and navigate your way around the cares of this world lonely. Beloved, you are not forsaken! You are a child of the Highest! Adopted into the beloved and accepted by Abba, Father! You don't have to choose Him because He already chose you! Choose to trust and believe His promises today!

Will you trust Him? Let every stronghold of fear be broken off your life and declare that your focus is centered on the love of God and His promises! Believe that every word He has spoken will accomplish what He purposed. There is nothing that can snatch you from the Father's hand or undermine His plan for you. Abba will carry out the work He began in you until completion! Just as every single raindrop and snowflake doesn't return to Him empty and without achieving His purpose for it, you can rest assured knowing that God's mission for you will manifest in its due season. Don't allow fear to hinder or lie to you anymore; instead, have faith, hope, and rest in God's love. Although we live in a broken world where pain and suffering exist, you have love, power, and a sound mind to live up in a down world and to be light in a dark world.

Isaiah 55:8-11, 1 John 3:1-3, 1 John 4:7-21,
Romans 8:14-17

What false beliefs do you have about God's love towards you? Write a love letter to God expressing your heart and embrace His love by etching the scriptures above on your heart. FEAR WILL NO LONGER TRAP YOU! Soak in the healing songs today!

"Reckless Love" (Cory Asbury)
"No Longer Slaves" (Jonathan David & Melissa Helser)
"No Bondage" (Jubilee Worship feat. Jennie O. & Anthony Brown)

Remember This...
ABBA FATHER LOVES YOU!

Day 5

*"Heal me, Lord, and I'll be healed.
Save me and I'll be saved, for you
are my heart's desire."*

Jeremiah 17:14 (CEB)

BEAUTIFULLY HEALED

There is no healing in blame. Let that sink in. Because it's easier to blame God and others for the pain you've endured, the broken relationships, deceit, manipulation, and everything else that has caused you to doubt everyone and every good thing, right? Although I can relate to these feelings, I must admit that you are wrong for feeling this way. I was crazy for feeling this way too. If you think you have a right to blame your offender and God for your condition when you have a choice to rise above every hurt, pain, damaging circumstance, guilt, and even the shame you didn't ask for, then you're deceived and highly mistaken. Healing begins when you relinquish your right to hold on to every grudge. Forgiveness is key to a life of faith and freedom. You have a choice to surrender the pain of your past and invite Jesus in to heal your present condition and heart. No, our Heavenly Father didn't orchestrate the pain, but the process of healing is so intentional. Don't ever doubt that God wasn't hurt by the things that hurt you. It says in His word that the Lord keeps track of your sorrows and collects all your tears in a bottle (*Psalms 56:8*). He knows everything about you, and He loves and cares too much to leave you the way you are. The question is, do you love and care about you enough to let it all go? Do you trust God, and will you call upon Him for rescue?

Being healed, cleansed, and made whole is a choice. Will you arise and decide, or are you comfortable sitting in your bed of affliction? I'll ask you again, beloved: What are you holding onto that you need to let go? Surrender. Often the breakthroughs you pray for come by releasing the one thing you fear losing the most. Are you holding on to anger, unforgiveness, resentment, control, guilt, shame, fear, unbelief, isolation? It is possible to hinder your ability to receive the beauty of healing and restoration God gives when you refuse to exchange them for the ashes and brokenness clenched tightly in your fists; not realizing the contribution you're making to your bondage by declining to discharge the chains you've gotten accustomed to wearing around your feet. I know because I too struggled with learning how to master the law of release. It can be hard and takes time, but it is possible. Ask God to apply the healing balm of His Holy Spirit over the wounds of your heart today, and to help you release everything not meant for you to hold. It is true that *"the heart that forgives is the heart that will live totally free from the pain of the past. And the heart that let's go is the heart that will know so much freedom."* My prayer is that you will have a heart like Jesus, one that loves and forgives even your enemies; one that no longer remembers the sting of heartaches and disappointments, and that loves unconditionally without fear of what man might do to you. That, my friend, is a heart that is beautifully healed by God.

Psalm 147:3

This may be a difficult task because it will require you to FEEL and DEAL with your emotions, but you can do it! Allow the Holy Spirit to search the crevices of your heart and uncover roots of bitterness and unforgiveness you have suppressed. Write what comes to mind then release it to God. He knows how to handle those offenses better than you ever will. Ask our loving Father to heal your heart and do your part by intentionally letting go of every chain that has held you bound.

"**A Heart That Forgives**" (Kevin LeVar)
"**Healer: I Believe You're My Healer**" (Kari Jobe)
"**We Need You Now: Heal the Land**" (Todd Gallberth)

Remember This...

HEALING IS YOUR PORTION

Day 6

"And be not conformed to this world: but be ye transformed by the renewing of your mind, that ye may prove what is that good, and acceptable, and perfect will of God."

Romans 12:2 (KJV)

BEAUTIFULLY TRANSFORMED

I know what you're thinking, *"I've heard this scripture a thousand times before."* But do you understand what it means? While this sinful world wants to stunt our growth and keep us wobbling in patterns of dysfunction, disobedience, immaturity, rebellion, and brokenness, God desires for us to be transformed more into the image and likeness of His Son, Jesus Christ. He wants us to be mature and whole. The world teaches us that change happens on the outside first and then the inside, but as

Believers, we should know that transformation is an inside process. The term "be" in this scripture means "to continue or remain as before" and insinuates that we were not created to *conform* to the patterns and socially acceptable behaviors of this world. We should *be* changed, and our thinking renewed, our character, and our nature must be established according to God's original design. You must take on the mind of Christ and look at life from God's viewpoint instead of this world's broken perspective.

The renewing of your mind involves learning God's will for you, His values, His desires, and His thoughts towards you. It requires asking the Lord to renew and elevate your understanding of how He operates so the Holy Spirit can repair the perception of your life, yourself, and others.

Then you will learn to know what God's good, acceptable, and *mature* will is for you.

Transformation is like the metamorphosis of a butterfly; it's such a complex but beautiful course. The struggle can get real, but remember that Jesus is very much real too! Perhaps, you have been resisting God in changing the way you think or wrestling with the enemy for control over your mind. Resist the devil and surrender to God. Be honest with yourself about where you are because it's challenging to change a problem when you don't admit its existence. Don't feel condemned or be ashamed of stinking thinking or the silent issues you've kept hidden from people. Remember, there's nothing you can hide from God.

Next, get informed! Your understanding is only limited to what you know. Knowledge is power, but the application of it is transformative! Faith comes by *hearing* the word of God. Get informed by reading the word of God and renewing your mind! Sit under sound leaders who feed your faith and care more about the development of your character and maturity in Christ. That is what real transformation is all about! It's not enough to be informed, be transformed! Win the battle over your mind by resisting evil thoughts before they become evident in your life. Declare today that you will never be the same, think the same, or live the same!

Romans 12:2, 2 Corinthians 3:18

What event or trauma may have damaged your belief system, the way you think? Do you remember or have you suppressed the memories of the seeds planted that birthed unhealthy thinking patterns and dysfunctional behaviors in your life? Identify the root, renounce it, repent for coming into agreement with the lies, and replace those seeds with the promises of God! Find scriptures relating to the mind to pray over your mind.

"Love Me Too Much" (Travis Greene)
"Never Be the Same" (Shana Wilson & Tasha Cobbs)

Remember This...
YOU HAVE THE MIND OF CHRIST

Day 7

"In His kindness God called you to share in His eternal glory by means of Christ Jesus. So, after you have suffered a little while, He will restore, support, and strengthen you, and He will place you on a firm foundation."

I Peter 5:10 (NLT)

BEAUTIFULLY RESTORED

Perhaps, you have read this scripture repeatedly, and on multiple occasions, the question you seem to always ask is, *"Lord, how long is a little while*?!" Let's be honest. Although we understand God's timing is different from ours, sometimes *His schedule* can feel like forever! Especially when you're tired of suffering! So, the question we normally ask is, "Why do we experience pain and suffering?" Well, pain is inevitable. There is no way we can live life free from pain. There are many reasons why we suffer through things. Suffering may be chastisement due to sin and rebellion; we partake in Christ's suffering for the Kingdom; suffering teaches us to give thanks for what we do have, and it also graces us with compassion to win souls for God. There's another side to the suffering we don't keep at the forefront of our minds—suffering for the sake of *maturing*. Rarely anybody gets overjoyed as James did about enduring hardships, but suffering is a vehicle God uses to develop, strengthen, prove, and settle His sons and daughters. He does this so that we become rooted in our faith, hope, trust, and dependence upon Him. James admonishes us in scripture to count it all joy when we are faced with affliction because it is building something in us! Perseverance and character! (see *James 1:2-4).*

If you allow God to change your perspective of suffering, it will transform your mind. Now, I'm not saying you should go and pray for more suffering or make decisions in life that create unnecessary pain, that's different. Instead, view suffering as a tool to sharpen, refine, perfect, and to keep you from stumbling. Suffering teaches us obedience to God—like it did for Jesus—self-control, and how much we don't want to live a life independent of Him. So, let me get to the point: suffering pain and losses in life, no matter the circumstances, can leave us broken and our souls in need of restoration. Whether you have strayed away from God and suffered as a result or if you're surrendered to God and partaking in Christ's suffering, the pain is inevitable. Period. If you never experience loss, though, you would never come to know our Heavenly Father as a Restorer. Through every circumstance, the reward is always *knowing HIM more.*

It's foolish to try and rebuild and restore in your strength what God can only build in His power. You should feel relieved of the pressure after reading that! The beauty of suffering is that it reveals your value and glory more than your life's successes ever will. Restoration reminds us of our worth and the value of what we carry. Sadly, our value isn't always visible until we've been broken, damaged, and the cost to put us back together is exposed. One thing is sure, the *Master Builder* knows what it cost to build you, and He's backing the financial cost to restore you. Remember, you can trust in God's faithfulness and stand on His promise that you are called to partake in His glory through Jesus Christ! The work is finished! It is my prayer that God will restore unto you the joy of your salvation and grant you a willing spirit to sustain you! *(Psalm 51:12).*

1 Peter 5:10, Psalms 23

Write a transparent love letter to God using scriptures from the bible regarding restoration. Pray for God to restore you, but most importantly, restore your relationship with Him (*this is your prayer*). Allow God's compassion to meet your confession. Then, simply REST in the Finished work of Jesus Christ!

"I Will Restore" (Keven LeVar)
"The Other Side" (Fred Jerkins)
"Finished Work" (William McDowell)

Remember This...

REST! THERE IS NO RESTORATION WITHOUT IT!

About the Author

Tacondra Brown is an Author, Writer, Coach, and Servant of the Lord who gives hope, healing, deliverance and transformation with the love and truth of the gospel of Jesus Christ. Vocally gifted, very insightful, and extremely compassionate, she is best known for her beautiful spirit, contagious presence, and down-to-earth personality. Tacondra has a straightforward, transparent, loving, and practical approach to ministering the gospel, advising, counseling, and coaching others through life-changing transformations, and she provides guidance in helping others write their God-given truths. Her ministry and message reach the hearts of all people, but especially women who suffer from devastating losses, barrenness, identity crisis, fear, guilt, shame, and feelings of inadequacy. Tacondra shares her testimony of how God transformed her from the pain of barrenness to a purpose-filled life. Her published books include: *Transformed from Pain to Purpose,* and *Beautifully Transformed: Discovering Beauty in The Beast,* and her current project titled *Breaking the Barren Spirit: From Nothing to Nations* where she invites readers into her story of brokenness and her beautiful transformation of becoming a glory carrier for God. Tacondra is graced with pleasant words and a healing anointing to bring hearts back to the Father, restoration and wholeness to many who are bound, broken, and wounded.

www.ingramcontent.com/pod-product-compliance
Lightning Source LLC
Chambersburg PA
CBHW060040040426
42331CB00032B/1940